How To Play
PIANO

A Complete Guide
for Absolute Beginners

Ben Parker

Author: Ben Parker

Editor: Alison McNicol

First published in 2013 by Kyle Craig Publishing

This version updated Dec 2014

Text and illustration copyright © 2013 Kyle Craig Publishing

Design and illustration: Julie Anson

Music set by Ben Parker using Sibelius software

ISBN: 978-1-908-707-16-1

A CIP record for this book is available from the British Library.

A Kyle Craig Publication
www.kyle-craig.com

Contents

Introduction

Welcome to **How To Play The Piano**. The piano is one of the most popular musical instruments to learn. Many beginners find it easy to pick out a simple tune quickly because the keys are right in front of them and the notes so accessible. Also included in this book is a step by step guide to reading music.

 ## Practice

Like any skill, playing an instrument takes a lot of practice. Practicing more regularly for shorter lengths of time is more effective than practicing for an hour or so just once a week.

The minimum amount would be around 15-20 minutes 3 to 4 times a week. The ideal amount would be 20 minutes a day, 7 days a week. Maybe set out a plan of your week and work out the best times to fit your practicing around the other things you do. The more your practice can become part of your weekly or daily routine the better.

It is the returning to the instrument that will make your practice time more worthwhile. So remember little and often is better than a lot, less often.

> *Remember,*
> ***little and often***
> *is best!*

Playing Position

You should always try to sit with your back straight on a suitable stool/chair. Your forearms should be at the same level as the keyboard. Your hands should never reach up to the keys. You may have to experiment with the height of your seat.

Hand Position

Your hands should be moved from the wrist. You should keep your wrists in line with your hands. Your fingers should be slightly bent and should adopt a 'half claw' position on the keys.

Your Fingers

The fingers of both your hands are numbered to help us know which fingers should play which notes. The thumb is number 1 on each hand:

Symbols in Music

The Clefs

There are two staves in all piano music. These are made up of 5 lines each. The top stave is for the **RIGHT HAND** and uses the **treble clef** at the beginning:

 The **treble clef** is for the **RIGHT HAND**

The bottom stave is for the **LEFT HAND** and uses the **bass clef** at the beginning:

 The **bass clef** is for the **LEFT HAND**

Time Signatures

Music is divided up into **bars**. Bars have a certain number of **beats**. The **time signature** is two numbers sat on top of each other at the beginning of every piece of music — the TOP number tells us how many beats there are in each bar:

 A time signature showing **FOUR** beats in each bar

 A time signature showing **THREE** beats in each bar

 A time signature showing **TWO** beats in each bar

Here's how it looks on the staves:

The Keyboard

Although you may recognize it instantly, the piano keyboard may be confusing for a beginner. It is made up of white and black keys — the black keys are grouped in pairs and in threes.

This regular pattern of black notes is repeated all the way along the keyboard and it helps us to work out where all the notes are. Almost like a map.

Let's Get Playing – The Middle C

To get us started, let's find the note **Middle C**. This is the white note to the left of the pair of black notes on your piano (often nearest to the lock for the piano lid).

Middle **C**

First of all let's see what the **Middle C** looks like in music — notice the small number 1 below it — this is there to remind us to play the **Middle C** with finger 1 (the thumb) of the right hand.

The note shown is a **WHOLE NOTE**. You count this for **FOUR** beats.

Middle C in the RIGHT HAND

Try playing two whole note **middle C**'s in a row. Count 1 as your thumb pushes down on the key then count to 4 before you play your next **C**:

Now lets try using the same note but with **quarter notes**. These last for 1 beat each so there are 4 of them in each bar:

New Note D In The Right Hand

Now let's try a new note!

Your new note **D** is played with the second finger of your right hand:

D in the RIGHT HAND

Step By Step

Playing With Your Left Hand

Now let's try playing with our left hand.

In the left hand, the **middle C** is also played with finger number 1 (the thumb). The left hand stave is written using a **bass clef**.

Middle C in the LEFT HAND

Counting 4 beats in each bar try your left hand **C** as quarter notes:

New Note B In The Left Hand

Your new note **B** is played with the second finger of your left hand:

Down And Out

Note Lengths

So far we have looked at **whole notes** (four beats) and **quarter notes** (1 beat).

Let's see the two other types of notes we'll use in this book — the **half note** (2 beats) and the **eighth note** (half a beat).

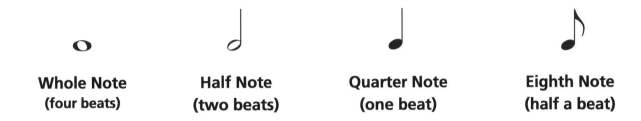

| Whole Note
(four beats) | Half Note
(two beats) | Quarter Note
(one beat) | Eighth Note
(half a beat) |

The next piece has both quarter notes and half notes in BOTH hands! Make sure you count carefully as you play — the main beat count is written above the treble clef to help you see where the notes are in the bar.

Turn Left, Turn Right

'Long Time Coming' has all your longer notes in. The whole note lasting for four beats and the half note lasting for two. Count carefully through this and be patient with those long notes!

Long Time Coming

New Note E In The Right Hand

E in the RIGHT HAND

 ## 3/4 or Waltz Time 1²³ 1²³ 1₂³

So far all of our music has been written with 4 beats to a bar. 4/4 is probably the most common time signature you will come across. Another time signature you will see a lot is 3/4 (three beats in a bar). Commonly known as **Waltz time** it was also a popular dance in the late 18th century.

$$\frac{3}{4}$$

The important thing to remember when counting and playing 3/4 time is to think of beat 1 as a STRONG beat whilst beats 2 & 3 are weaker. In the exercise below the counts are written above the music with beat 1 in **BOLD** to help show the stronger beat. Try playing the note on the first beat a little bit louder than the following 2. The last note is a dotted half note — you play this for 3 beats.

New Note A In The Left Hand

A in the LEFT HAND

Dance Class

New Note F In The Right Hand

F in the RIGHT HAND

New Note G In The Left Hand

G in the LEFT HAND

Try this short piece. It will help you get used to your new notes

Up And Down

Rests

Rests tell us when not to play. Like notes, they last for different lengths of time. These different lengths are shown as different symbols:

Whole note rest
(4 beats or
one whole bar)

Half note rest
(2 beats)

Quarter note rest
(1 beat)

Eighth note rest
($\frac{1}{2}$ beat)

Try **'Take A Break'** — it has whole, half and quarter note rests so make sure you count through the bars carefully.

Take A Break

The well-known tune for **'Mary Had A Little Lamb'** is played here in the right hand only. Whole bar rests are used to tell us to rest the left hand throughout. It also has your new note **G** in the right hand.

G in the RIGHT HAND

Mary Had A Little Lamb

Twinkle Twinkle

On And Off

Moving Between Hands

In **'London Bridge Is Falling Down'** there is more movement between the hands. Make sure you keep the fingers of each hand over the top of the notes they play.

London Bridge Is Falling Down

Yankee Doodle

Changing Hand Positions

So far we have stuck closely to having the thumbs of each hand covering the **middle C** note.
Now let's try moving the left hand position so the left hand thumb now plays the **lower G** note.

How this looks on the left hand (**bass clef**) stave with the little finger (number 5) playing the
C below.

At the end of line two of **'Row, Row'** you'll see a **tie** (curved line) between two notes. This joins them together (two dotted half notes tied = 6 beats).

Row, Row

Using Both Hands At The Same Time

Now let's try a very simple exercise to get you used playing with both hands at the same time. Remember your fingering for your left hand notes. Make sure you start with your left hand little finger (finger 5) on the **C** below **middle C**.

Now let's add some movement to your left hand part, keeping the right hand the same:

In this last exercise, both hands move around quite a bit. Take it really slowly to begin with then speed up gradually as your confidence increases.

Rolling Hills

Sunrise

Slow Dance

Eighth Notes

So far we've only used whole notes, half notes and quarter notes. Our new note length is an **eighth** note. This is also known as a **quaver**. These last for half a beat. When counting eighth notes use 1 & 2 & 3 & 4 &. This will help you with the rhythm.

Note that your left hand position changes back to thumb on **middle C** in '**Hush Little Baby**'.

Hush Little Baby

Oranges And Lemons

Watch out for the dotted quarter notes in **'Jingle Bells'**. These last for one and a half beats and when followed by an eighth note add a nice 'skip' to the rhythm of this well known melody.

Jingle Bells

Changing Hand Positions Within A Piece

Sometimes you need to shift hand positions within a piece. Try the piece below and note the left hand position change in the 3rd line.

Au Clair De La Lune

left hand position change

left hand change back

The Other Notes

There are other notes on your treble and bass clef staves as well as the notes you can play with each of the five fingers of your two hands. As your playing develops you'll need these notes to play more difficult pieces.

Notice that the notes are on the lines or in the spaces between them. To help us remember these other notes we have some handy fun phrases:

The Notes on the Right Hand Stave (Treble Clef)

Notes on the lines

E   G   B   D   F

Notes in the spaces

F   A   C   E

The Notes On The Left Hand Stave (Bass Clef)

Notes on the lines

Notes in the spaces

G B D F A

A C E G

Watch out for the fingering and the hand position changes in this piece. Bar 6 (and bar 14) requires you to tuck your thumb under the other fingers of the right hand to play the **B** note. In the next bar (and bar 15) finger 3 then moves over the thumb to play the **G** on the way back down.

What Shall We Do With The Drunken Sailor?

Playing Chords

In most pop music today the piano or keyboard is often used as an accompanying chordal instrument where the player will use both hands to play the chord progression or 'pattern' of the song. To illustrate this, we'll be using fingerings to help map out the position of your fingers.

Unlike the more 'classical' approach where the right hand plays the melody and always has a defined position, this pop style requires frequent position changes of the right hand. Let's start by looking at the hand positions for your three main chords, **C**, **F** and **G**.

The hand position for your **C** chord shown below shows a move away from the traditional '1 finger per key' positioning. Your second finger now stretches along to play the **E** note, whilst your 4th finger moves up to the **G**.

Chord C

Chord F

In your **F** chord, your thumb remains on **C**, your 3rd finger plays the **F** note whilst your 5th finger plays the **A**. This is to help you move smoothly from the **C** chord. Your left hand uses finger 2 to play the **F** bass note.

Chord G

And finally for your **G** chord your thumb now moves down to play the **B** note below **middle C**, your 2nd finger plays the **D** note whilst your 5th finger plays the **G**.

Let's Play Chords!

You may recognize the sound of these three chords when played together. They make up the 'three chord trick' made infamous by blues and rock n roll. Play them slowly to start with then try a bit more movement as you go:

Exercise 1

Exercise 2

12 Bar Blues

Rockin' And Rollin'

Quiz!

NAME THAT NOTE!

- -

- -

- -

- -

- -

- -

How many beats do each of these notes last for?

HALF/ONE/TWO/FOUR   **HALF/ONE/TWO/FOUR**   **HALF/ONE/TWO/FOUR**   **HALF/ONE/TWO/FOUR**

Quiz!

Can you fill in the correct **RIGHT HAND NOTE** names on the keys above?

- -

Can you name the **CHORDS** above?

Right Hand Notes

Left Hand Notes

MORE GREAT MUSIC BOOKS FROM KYLE CRAIG!

How To Play UKULELE — A Complete Guide for Absolute Beginners

978-1-908-707-08-6

My First UKULELE — Learn to Play: Kids

978-1-908-707-11-6

Easy UKULELE Tunes

978-1-908707-37-6

How To Play GUITAR — A Complete Guide for Absolute Beginners

978-1-908-707-09-3

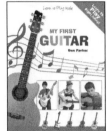

My First GUITAR — Learn to Play: Kids

978-1-908-707-13-0

Easy GUITAR Tunes

978-1-908707-34-5

How To Play KEYBOARD — A Complete Guide for Absolute Beginners

978-1-908-707-14-7

My First KEYBOARD — Learn to Play: Kids

978-1-908-707-15-4

Easy KEYBOARD Tunes

978-1-908707-35-2

How To Play PIANO — A Complete Guide for Absolute Beginners

978-1-908-707-16-1

My First PIANO — Learn to Play: Kids

978-1-908-707-17-8

Easy PIANO Tunes

978-1-908707-33-8

How To Play HARMONICA — A Complete Guide for Absolute Beginners

978-1-908-707-28-4

My First RECORDER — Learn to Play: Kids

978-1-908-707-18-5

Easy RECORDER Tunes

978-1-908707-36-9

How To Play BANJO — A Complete Guide for Absolute Beginners

978-1-908-707-19-2

The GUITAR Chord Dictionary

978-1-908707-39-0

The UKULELE Chord Dictionary

978-1-908707-38-3

Printed in Great Britain
by Amazon